SEASONAL
wreaths

SEASONAL
wreaths

Susanna Morrison

EBURY PRESS
LONDON

For my daughter Polly

First published in 1997

1 3 5 7 9 10 8 6 4 2

Text and arrangements copyright © Susanna Morrison 1997
Photographs copyright © Sandra Lane 1997

First published in the United Kingdom in 1997 by Ebury Press
Random House, 20 Vauxhall Bridge Road, London SW1V 2SA

Random House Australia (Pty) Limited
20 Alfred Street, Milsons Point, Sydney,
New South Wales 2061, Australia

Random House New Zealand Limited
18 Poland Road, Glenfield, Auckland 10, New Zealand

Random House South Africa (Pty) Limited
Endulini, 5a Jubilee Road, Parktown 2193, South Africa

Random House UK Limited Reg. No. 954009

A CIP catalogue record for this book is available from the British Library.

ISBN 0 09 185356 7

Edited by Gillian Haslam
Designed by Christine and Paul Wood
Photography by Sandra Lane
Styling by Wei Tang

Printed and bound in Singapore by Tien Wah Press

Contents

introduction

The most enjoyable aspect of working with flowers is that no week is ever the same. Each season brings its own joys. Even now, with so many flowers flown in from around the world, there is nothing more wonderful than the first box of home-grown ranunculus appearing in the market. With their tissue-paper petals and jewel-like colours they never cease to make me smile. Or imagine the pleasure of gathering armfuls of rosehips, blackberries and boughs of sunset-coloured leaves on a crisp autumn afternoon. It was with these thoughts in mind that I began to write this book.

Though we tend to associate wreaths with Christmas, as you will see in this book, they come in many guises and can be used for so many different occasions.

A wreath is simply a circle of a decorative nature and can be made from almost any material you wish to use. When I began this book, the notion of designing over thirty different wreaths was quite daunting! However it quickly became apparent that there are so many aspects to wreath-making and so many variations and materials that can be used, and it was not long before I was having to choose which designs to include and which to omit.

For centuries wreaths have been used in one form or another, from the Roman era when a garland of laurel leaves was used to adorn the head of the victor of the games, through to Victorian times when wreaths of dried flowers and herbs

were hung on the door to ward off evil sprits. The circle symbolises continuity, rebirth and fertility and is a prominent symbol in many religious ceremonies, not least the gold wedding band we exchange when marrying today.

Many wreaths in this book would make ideal presents, perhaps as a house-warming gift or specially designed with the recipient in mind: a garden wreath of seeds, plant tags and twine to be hung in the greenhouse, for example, or a wreath made from tiny silver pill boxes to store jewellery in. Wreaths can be as simple or as elaborate as you wish. Whether as a permanent decoration or as an arrangement for a special occasion, the possibilities are endless.

I hope that as you look through this book you will be inspired to make some of the wreaths featured, but also to use the designs as a springboard for your own ideas.

Susanna Morrison

spring

Spring is a magical time. As the world wakes from its winter hibernation, branches hang heavy with blossom and daffodils splash the countryside with their cheerful trumpets of yellow. There is a feeling of rebirth and renewal, as the perfume of hyacinth and narcissi fills the air and the birds sing in the pale morning light.

valentine wreaths

Extravagant, opulent and sumptuous, these Valentine's wreaths would win over anyone's heart. Thick clusters of sweetly fragrant blooms in sugary pinks, deep reds and creamy whites tightly massed together create a rich tapestry of roses. The smaller wired hearts would make a beautiful gift for a table setting, or to adorn a special present. Both wreaths would dry very well, providing a lasting memento of a romantic day.

MATERIALS

40 cm (16 in) heart-shaped foam wreath

pink or red dyed lichen
(see Suppliers on page 119)

medium gauge stub wires

20 of each of the following or similar roses: *Vicki Brown, Valerie, Bianca, Wendy, Red Ace, Grand Prix*

1 Condition the roses by removing the foliage from the lower part of the stems and then cutting stems at an angle. Place in cool water almost up to their heads and leave to stand for at least 12 hours.

2 Soak the wreath base in water for a few minutes. Secure clumps of lichen to the wreath with stub wires bent into a 'U' shape. Cover the inner and outer edges of the plastic base until only the foam is visible.

3 Starting with the largest roses, in this case the red *Grand Prix*, cut the stems about 7.5 cm (3 in) from the head and push into the foam, arranging them equally around the wreath.

4 Add the white *Bianca* roses and then continue to add roses, spacing the colours evenly. Fill in gaps with spray roses until all the foam is covered. Spray with a fine mist of water.

small hearts

MATERIALS

2 stub wires

1 m (1 yard) organza or wired ribbon

5 stems of *Red Ace* spray roses

1 Bend one stub wire into a 'V' shape and the other to form the top of the heart. Tie a piece of ribbon 50 cm (20 in) long to the 'V' at the top of the heart.

2 Gently thread the rosebuds through the wire at the base of the petals, taking care not to split the buds.

3 Push the rosebuds along the wire. Ensure both wires are tightly packed with flowers. This is important if you intend to keep the wreath as roses shrink considerably as they dry. Continue until only 2.5 cm (1 in) of wire is showing at each end.

4 Join the two wires together by gently pushing the exposed wires into the rosebud on the other wire to form a heart. Finish by adding the bow.

Easter wreath

The electrifying orange and mauve of the crocuses, the deep pinks and rich blues of the hyacinths – it can be no coincidence that after the long, cold winter, the flowers of spring have a radiancy all of their own. With the bright yellow daffodils, speckled quails' eggs, tails of catkins and the delicately scented paper whites, this wreath represents all the vibrancy of spring. It would make an ideal Easter gift, perhaps substituting the real eggs for chocolate ones, or baskets of sugared ones. A larger version would look stunning as a font decoration, a ray of sunshine after the absence of flowers during Lent.

MATERIALS

3 duck eggs (available from delicatessens)

8 quails' eggs (available from delicatessens)

medium and fine gauge stub wires

2 bunches of grape hyacinths

2 bunches of daffodils

2 bunches of yellow ranunculus

1 bunch of paper whites

30 cm (12 in) wet foam wreath base

small selection of feathers

selection of spring foliage, such as catkins, blossom, forsythia, pussywillow and young beech

3 lengths of trailing ivy

sharp scissors

1 First, blow the eggs (see step 1, page 33) and then wire them carefully (see page 114).

2 Wire grape hyacinths, using a double leg mount. Also wire the daffodils, ranunculus and paper whites (see pages 112 and 113).

3 Soak the foam base in water for a few minutes, and starting on one side of the wreath, group the duck eggs together. Using these as a starting point, add the foliage and flowers, working around the wreath in two crescent shapes until the two sides meet.

4 Add the quails' eggs and feathers at intervals. Twist in the trails of ivy. Give the whole wreath a generous spray of water to complete.

christening wreath

There is something indescribably beautiful about the baptism of a young child, from the crisp, cotton gown to the symbolic lighting of the candle. This wreath has been designed for a young boy's christening in spring. Set against the strong blue tones of the hydrangea heads, grape hyacinths, bluebells and lilac, the creamy white puffs of ranunculus look like soft clouds.

MATERIALS

2 hydrangea heads
1 bunch of rosemary
5 branches of blossom
10 stems of guelder rose
1 bunch of lilac
15 cream *Eskimo* roses
1 bunch of ranunculus
3 stems of sea holly
3 bunches of blue scillas
3 bunches of white scillas
5 bunches of grape hyacinths
medium gauge stub wires
36 cm (14 in) wet foam base

1 Condition the flowers and branches in water (see pages 110-111).

2 Divide each hydrangea head into three and wire the stems (see pages 112-114).

3 Soak the wreath base in a bowl of water for a few minutes. Arrange sprigs of rosemary, blossom. guelder rose and lilac around the outer rim of the base. Continue until the entire base is covered, providing a green foliage canvas on which to add the flowers.

4 Push the wired hydrangeas deep into the foliage at intervals.

5 Add the roses, ranunculus and sea holly evenly around the wreath. Complete by adding the scillas and grape hyacinths. Give the wreath a good spray with water.

candelabra wreath

Ranunculus are a member of the buttercup family and, with some of the varieties, the similarity is quite apparent. However, unlike buttercups, ranunculus come in the most glorious array of colours and are almost jewel-like in their intensity. Ranging from scarlet to peach, acid yellow to deep purple, the colours of this spring flower make it an ideal choice for party arrangements.

This wreath has been designed to encircle the base of a candelabra and would make a fantastic table centre for a carnival themed evening, with the colours of the wreath echoing the diamonds of a harlequin.

MATERIALS
10 bunches of ranunculus
3 bunches of narcissi
20 orange roses
florists' scissors
medium gauge stub wires (optional)
25 cm (10 in) wet foam base

1 Condition all the flowers (see pages 110-111). The ranunculus should be conditioned in a similar way to tulips. The narcissi should be conditioned separately.

2 Soak the wreath base in water for a few minutes.

3 The aim is to create a solid mass of flowers, so it is useful to begin by using the narcissi to give an outline to the wreath. Cut 8 narcissi to the height of the finished arrangement (approximately 15 cm/6 in). Push them vertically around the inner rim of the wreath base (you may need to wire the stems of the narcissi if they are small).

4 Cut a further 12 narcissi to a height of approximately 14 cm (5 in) and push these in horizontally around the outer rim of the base.

5 Cut the remaining narcissi to a height of approximately 15 cm (6 in) and push in at an angle around the centre of the base. This will give a skeleton guideline from which to build the wreath.

6 Add the roses evenly throughout the wreath. Then, working in sections, fill in the entire wreath with ranunculus. These have fairly fragile stems so be careful as you push them into the foam.

7 Finish the wreath with a good spray of water, remembering to protect the table surface if it is damaged by water.

plant wreath

After months of grey days and foggy mornings, spring arrives and with it the first bulbs and plants of the year. It can be no coincidence that spring flowers have such vibrancy, from the bright mauves and oranges of the crocus, the acid yellows of the daffodil and the multi-coloured hues of the polyanthus.

This wreath is simple both in its construction and its contents, but it would guarantee to lift anyone's spirits after a long, cold winter. Ideal as Mother's Day gift, the planted wreath has an advantage over fresh flowers in that it will last a lot longer, and being simple to assemble, could easily be made by a child.

MATERIALS
An old 30 cm (12 in) wet foam base
12 polyanthus or any small annuals, such as pansies, primroses or petunias

1 First, remove all the old florists' foam from the wreath so you are left with the plastic base.

2 Take the plants out of their pots and gently push them into the plastic base. Continue to add the plants, packing them tightly until the whole base has been filled.

3 Water well every two to three days, removing dead heads and leaves as they appear. If you are placing the wreath on a surface which might be damaged by drops of water, sit the wreath on a tray or large platter.

mosaic wreath

Mosaic has been used as a form of decoration for many centuries. First used by the Romans in their palaces and later revived by the Italians to decorate their churches, it is still very popular today.

Although traditionally made from pieces of marble, many other materials can be used. This wreath is made from a combination of glass mosaic squares mixed with broken terracotta, china and coloured glass. You could also include broken shells, coins, egg shells or pebbles. This wreath would look particularly pretty in a bathroom filled with shells, natural sponges or driftwood.

1 Pack the wire wreath base with crumpled up newspaper.

2 Make up the plaster of Paris according to packet's instructions. Taking one strip of calico at a time, dip it in the plaster and then wrap it around the wire frame. Continue until the whole frame is covered. Leave to dry for a few hours, and then repeat with another layer of plaster and fabric to give a good firm base.

3 On a flat surface arrange your pieces of mosaic in a circle to give an idea of the finished pattern. It is easier to do this now rather than when you are working on the wreath.

4 Working in small sections at a time, cover the base with tile grout, and press the mosaic pieces into the grout. Continue until the whole wreath is covered. Allow to dry.

5 Fill in any gaps with a little extra grout and, using the cloth, wipe the mosaic pieces clean . Allow to dry.

6 Dilute the paint with two parts white spirit to one part paint and brush generously all over the wreath. Wipe any excess off the mosaic pieces.

7 With the glue gun, 'pipe' glue around selected pieces of mosaic. Once it is dry, paint with a gold felt-tip pen.

MATERIALS
25 cm (10 in) wire base
old newspaper
old tea towel or calico cut into 2.5 cm (1 in) strips
1 litre (1½ pints) plaster of Paris
selection of small pieces of broken china and glass
selection of coloured glass mosaic squares
ready-made tile grout
soft cloth
enamel paint
white spirit
paint brush
glue gun
gold felt-tip pen

sweet wreath

MATERIALS
30 cm (12 in) foam base
kitchen foil
sticky tape
assorted sweets
glue gun or tube of all-purpose glue
cocktail sticks or toothpicks (optional)

This is a fun wreath that would make a wonderful centrepiece for a children's party. Based on the same principle as the shell wreath on page 48, the sweets are glued onto a solid base. You can be as inventive as you like, using sticks of rock, jelly shapes, liquorice sweets and foil-wrapped ones. Larger supermarkets often have an amazing array of sweets available to buy by the weight – some are so fantastic it is hard to believe they are edible! How about filling the centre of the wreath with squishy marshmallows, lollipops or little going-home presents?

1 Cover the foam base with crumpled kitchen foil, securing it at the back with sticky tape. You could also use coloured cellophane or tissue paper if you wish.

2 Working on just a small section of the wreath at a time, carefully glue on the sweets, taking care not to place identical or similarly coloured sweets next to each other.

3 Continue gluing sweets until the whole wreath is covered. Then add a few more sweets to the top of the wreath to add more depth.

4 If you are making this for a children's party, use only foil- or paper-wrapped sweets and attach them using toothpicks. Take care that young children do not harm themselves with the toothpicks.

feather wreath

The circle symbolises eternal life and continuity, so it is rather apt to make a circle of feathers and eggs, with eggs representing the beginning of life and the shaded feathers depicting continuity, replacing old with new. Birds line their homes with feathers creating their own version of a feathered wreath each time they make a nest. You could use any type of feathers – peacock, pigeon, hen or even ostrich!

MATERIALS

5 hen's eggs

darning needle

small bowl

medium gauge stub wires

block of florists' foam or polystyrene

enamel and emulsion paint in
5 different colours

paint brushes

white spirit (for cleaning brushes)

5 birch or other flexible branches

reel wire

scissors

selection of coloured and natural
feathers, approximately 140 in total

5 x 50 cm (20 in) lengths of narrow satin
ribbon

glue gun or tube of all-purpose glue

1 m (1 yard) net ribbon, 5 cm (2 in)
wide

1 m (1 yard) webbing, 5 cm (2 in) wide

1 First, prepare the eggs by blowing them. Wash the shell thoroughly and, using a darning needle, make a small hole at each end. Push the needle through the egg to break the yolk. Hold the egg over a bowl and blow hard through one end until the yolk and white have emptied out through the other hole. Rinse the eggs carefully and dry the shells.

2 To paint the eggs, push one end of a stub wire through the small hole at the base of the egg. Push the other end of the wire into a block of florists' foam – this makes it easier to paint the egg without smudging. Carefully paint each egg with a different colour and leave to dry thoroughly.

3 Join two birch branches together so that the top half of the first branch overlaps the bottom half of the second branch. Bind the branches together securely with reel wire.

4 Continue to bind together the branches with reel wire, pulling in the twigs and overlapping each one with the previous, to create a solid base approximately 30 cm (12 in) in diameter.

5 Select three or four feathers, bunch them together and bind to the base with reel wire. Do not cut the wire but continue to add small bunches of feathers, overlapping them on the previous feathers. Angle some of the feathers slightly to cover the edges of the wreath. Continue until the whole wreath is covered.

6 Tie two of the eggs with lengths of narrow ribbon, then glue all the eggs to the wreath using a glue gun or all-purpose glue.

7 Tie the net and webbing into large bows and wire to the bottom of the wreath. Finally, attach the remaining thin satin ribbons behind the bows.

summer

As the days grow longer and warmer, the buttercups and poppies blow in the breeze, rustling among the golden ears of corn. Summer is the season of flowers in all their glorious abundance. Long balmy evenings and the heady scent of peonies, phlox and honeysuckle – it is hard to think of a more enchanting time of year.

sunflower wreath

There is no more beautiful a sight than the French Provençal sunflower fields in mid July. With acre upon acre of heavy yellow heads nodding towards the sun, the glorious vibrancy of the sunflower literally shines out at you, cheering up even the dullest day.

This arrangement would make a beautiful hoop to be carried by a bridesmaid at a summer wedding or a wonderful garland for the reception door. A smaller version without the sunflowers could be made as a garland head-dress.

MATERIALS
2 large buckets
newspaper
10 sunflowers
8 yellow roses
10 stems of yellow alstroemeria
10 stems of hypericum
10 stems of 'Yellow Dot' spray roses
1 bunch of corn
mixed summer foliage
8 branches of small leafed trailing ivy
sharp florists' scissors
heavy/medium and fine gauge stub wires
34 cm (14 in) plastic hoop (available from florists, or you could use a child's hula hoop)
green wiring tape
raffia

1 Condition the flowers by stripping away the lower leaves and cutting the stems at an angle before placing them in deep water for at least 12 hours. It may be necessary to wrap the sunflower heads loosely in newspaper to protect them while they are being conditioned, and prevent the heads flopping.

2 Cut the sunflowers and yellow roses approximately 10 cm (4 in) from the head and wire them using gauge wire (see page 113).

3 Cutting the rest of the flowers to a similar length, arrange them into 30 mixed bunches. Wire each bunch together. Cut the corn to 10 cm (4 in) and wire these together in bunches of four or five ears.

4 Starting with a sunflower, tape this firmly to the hoop using the wiring tape. Ensure that the wire is covered before adding a mixed bunch of flowers. Then add a bunch of corn, a rose, another mixed bunch and a sunflower. Continue with this sequence around the hoop until just a 10 cm (4 in) gap remains. Angle the flowers as you work so that all the sides of the hoop are covered. This is particularly important if it is to be carried by a bridesmaid.

5 To finish the hoop, add a large raffia bow at the top.

6 To make a head-dress, twist together 2 medium gauge wires to form a circle the circumference of the bridesmaid's head. Use a similar method to the hoop, but wire each flower and leaf individually. Omit the sunflowers as they are too big. However, you could substitute miniature yellow gerbera.

summer berries

As the late summer sun sets, it leaves behind a rosy glow that is echoed in the rich reds, pinks and amber hues of this berry and fruit wreath. This is ideal as a decorative centrepiece for a lavish summer buffet or high tea, surrounding an elegant cake stand or an ice bowl infused with rose petals.

At this time of the year summer berries are plentiful, so the more variation you can include, the more spectacular the wreath will be. Please remember that this wreath is not suitable for eating.

MATERIALS

25 cm (10 in) foam base

plastic food wrap

2 packets of cocktail sticks or toothpicks

selection of summer fruit and berries, such as:
kiwano (horned melon)
5 yellow plums
5 red plums
2 small apples
7 kumquats
2 punnets of strawberries
2 punnets of blackberries
1 punnet of raspberries
1 punnet of blueberries
1 punnet of cape gooseberries
1 punnet of cranberries
2 punnets of redcurrants

1 Wrap the foam base in a single layer of plastic wrap. This should prevent the base from becoming soggy and ensure the fruit lasts longer.

2 Starting with the kiwano, or your largest fruit, arrange around the wreath and secure to the base with cocktail sticks. For the larger fruit you may need two or three sticks. Follow with the plums, apples and then the kumquats.

3 For the berries you will only need one toothpick, or half a cocktail stick, for each berry. Starting with the strawberries, pin these to the base followed by the remaining berries. Finally, arrange the stems of redcurrants around the top.

vegetable wreath

MATERIALS

36 cm (14 in) wet foam wreath base

plastic food wrap

selection of the following miniature
vegetables:
1 packet of small leafed curly kale
1 head of broccoli
1 head of cauliflower
6 bell peppers
6 miniature aubergines (eggplants)
1 punnet of cherry tomatoes
1 punnet of pearl onions or shallots
3 chilli peppers
12 Brussels sprouts
2 bunches of salad or spring onions
9 miniature turnips
2 bunches of miniature carrots
1 bunch of radishes
1 fennel bulb
medium gauge stub wires

It is hard to pinpoint when vegetables first became popular in floral design, certainly many people have taken credit for it. I like to think that it was Uncle Monty in the film *Withnail and I*, who wore a radish as a buttonhole, and very charming he looked too! He believed that vegetables were infinitely more beautiful than flowers.

Though I would not go as far as to agree with him, with so many exotic and unusual vegetables available from all over the world it is possible to make some wonderful arrangements just using vegetables. This wreath is based around many of the miniature varieties of vegetables that are now available. It is intended to be purely decorative.

1 Cover the wreath base with a layer of plastic wrap.

2 Taking bunches of three kale leaves at a time and wire together using a double leg mount (see page 112). Push these in all the way around the outer and inner edge of the base.

3 Break the broccoli and cauliflower into florets. Wire all the vegetables individually, with the exception of the turnips, carrots and radishes which should be wired into bunches of three. Cut the fennel bulb in half and wire.

4 Starting with the bunches of vegetable, position them at an angle around both sides of the wreath, overlapping each bunch, and secure with hairpins of stub wire.

5 Position the two wired fennel halves at the base of the wreath.

6 Using the remaining vegetables, build up the wreath until the entire base is covered, mixing textures, colours and varieties.

7 Spray the wreath with a fine mist of water and keep in a cool place until you plan to use it.

lavender wreath

Lavender is renowned for its heavenly scent. Simple in its design and construction, this wreath would look stunning hung against a pine wardrobe or above a chest of drawers and would make any room smell wonderful.

It is easy to dry the flowers. Simply pick the lavender on a dry day and hang small bunches in a warm dry place, such as an airing cupboard, until they are completely dry. It is important to pick fairly young flowers otherwise they will drop. The scent of the lavender should remain for several months, however you can always add a few drops of lavender oil to enhance it.

MATERIALS
30 small bunches of lavender
scissors
reel wire
25 cm (10 in) wire wreath base
1 m (1 yard) raffia
1 m (1 yard) red paper ribbon

1 Cut the stems of each bunch of lavender to a length of 10 cm (4 in).

2 Using reel wire, take one bunch at a time and bind it to the wire frame, working around the base in a spiral until all the lavender has been used.

3 Plait the raffia together and 'stitch' it to the inside of the wreath using a length of reel wire.

4 Finally, tie the red paper ribbon into a large bow and carefully wire to the top of the wreath.

fresh herb wreath

MATERIALS

25 cm (10 in) foam base

medium gauge stub wires

plastic food wrap

5 garlic heads

10 chillies

2 bunches of thyme

1 bunch of rosemary

2 bunches of sage

raffia

2 branches of bay

bun or carpet moss

hessian bow (optional)

This herb wreath is a wonderful way of capturing the aromatic flavours and scents of summer. Made when herbs are in abundance, this wreath will dry to provide an evocative memory of balmy summer days. All the herbs used in this wreath dry well and, as they are tied in small bunches, can easily be replaced as they are used. Other herbs to consider using include oregano, mint and lemon grass.

1 Make a hook using stub wire (see page 115) and position on the back of the wreath. Cover the entire wreath base with a single layer of plastic wrap.

2 Wire the garlic heads and chillies (see page 113) and arrange around the base.

3 Using strands of raffia, tie the thyme, rosemary and sage into small bunches of three or four sprigs. Thread a stub wire through the back of the raffia and bend to form a hairpin. Push the bunches firmly into the wreath between the garlic and the chillies.

4 Strip the bay leaves from the branches and wire together in groups of three or four leaves. Push into the wreath between the bunches of herbs.

5 Finish by covering any visible wreath base with clumps of moss, held in place with hairpins of wire.

6 If you wish, add a raffia or hessian bow as a finishing touch.

shell wreath

After a long summer's walk along the coast or when returning from holiday with a suitcase of mementoes from the beach, what better way to preserve those happy memories than by turning your finds into a pretty shell wreath. You could also include pieces of driftwood, star fish, dried seaweed and pebbles.

MATERIALS
hardboard or thick cardboard
dry foam florists' ring
scissors or saw
glue gun or tube of all-purpose glue
masking tape
picture hook
assortment of shells and other beach 'finds'
satin varnish
paintbrush

1 Using the dry foam ring as a template, draw around it onto the hardboard or cardboard and then cut out a circle to fit the back of the ring.

2 With the glue gun or all-purpose glue, stick the hardboard base to the foam ring and then bind with masking tape to form a secure base for your wreath. Attach a picture hook at the back from which to hang it.

3 Next, arrange the shells along the top of the base, securing them to the dry foam using a glue gun.

4 Continue adding the shells and other materials along the outside edge and then along the inside, covering any gaps with smaller shells and pebbles.

5 Coat the entire wreath with two coats of satin varnish, allowing the first coat to dry thoroughly before applying the second.

summer table centre

MATERIALS
12 pink peonies
12 dark pink roses
mixed summer foliage
20 stems of lady's mantle (alchemilla)
10 stems of cow parsley
10 stems of mauve sweetpeas
10 stems of lily of the valley
3 stems of cream lisianthus
florists' scissors
36 cm (14 in) wet foam base

The flowers available around the time of the summer solstice are some of the most beautiful. Such is the abundance of colour and fragrance that we are almost spoilt for choice. This summer arrangement incorporates flowers that depict the typical colours of a herbaceous border with its mauves, powder blues and soft pinks.

Ideal as a table centre, you can almost imagine the fine linen table cloth laden with scones, strawberries and cream and bone china pots of Earl Grey tea under the dappled shade of a willow tree.

1 Condition all the flowers and foliage (see pages 110-111 for details). Soak the wreath base in a bowl of water for a few minutes.

2 Arrange the peonies and roses at intervals on the wreath base, angling each flower slightly and bearing in mind that the table centre will be seen from all angles.

3 Cut the smaller flowers to 15 cm (6 in). Add sprigs of foliage and smaller flowers around the outside of the base. Angle them down to hide the base.

4 Add the remaining flowers and foliage, building up the arrangement as you go. Finish with a spray of water. If necessary, place the wreath on a plate so that water will not damage the table.

bridesmaid's basket

There is nothing more romantic than a summer wedding, when the roses are in full bloom, the evenings are long and the scent of the sweet peas and honeysuckle mingles with the smell of freshly cut hay.

Young bridesmaids are one of the most charming aspects of any wedding, and give florists an ideal opportunity to indulge in fairytale fantasies, whether it is a scented pomander, a pretty ribboned hoop or a flower basket such as this. Filled with pink and white squares of nougat and bedecked with tiny ribbon bows, this little basket is light enough for any little girl to carry as she follows the bride down the aisle.

MATERIALS

medium and fine gauge wires

a small wicker basket approximately
24 cm (9 in) long by 18 cm (7 in) wide

14 *Porcelain* spray roses

20 grape hyacinths

14 sweetpea heads

20 small ivy leaves

10 rose leaves

3 m (3¾ yards) fine ribbon

florists' wiring tape

nougat, rose petal confetti or a small toy

1 Bend a medium gauge wire around the rim of half the basket. (You may need to join on an extra piece to give you the correct length.) Cut another piece the same length. These will provide the base wire on which to make your garland.

2 Wire each flower and leaf individually (see page 112).

3 Cut six 28 cm (11 in) pieces of ribbon, tie into tiny bows and wire using fine gauge wire.

4 Starting with a rosebud, tape it into the medium gauge wire using florists' wiring tape, add a sweetpea head, a grape hyacinth, an ivy leaf, bow, rosebud and so forth, taping each one as you go. Continue along the wire, leaving a gap of 2.5 cm (1 in) at the end. Remember to save half the flowers and leaves for the second wire.

5 Using fine gauge wire, carefully 'sew' the garland onto the rim of half the basket. Gently angle the flowers to cover any wires.

6 Repeat the process for the other side of the basket. It is easier to make the garland in two pieces, as the flowers can be heavy and without the support of the basket, a longer garland can be difficult to work with.

7 Wrap the remaining ribbon around the handle, finishing with a bow on either side. Fill the basket with sweets, rose petal confetti or a little toy.

autumn

The richness of autumn with its bounty of fruits, berries and nuts is a time for reaping the harvest – a season filled with the aromatic crackle of bonfires and roasting chestnuts, when the leaves turn a wonderful kaleidoscope of reds, oranges and yellows. Autumn is a time of mellowness and making ready for winter.

3 orange peppers or gourds
7 cabbage leaves
medium gauge stub wires
30 cm (12 in) wet foam base
12 large orange roses
15 stems of Singapore orchids
1 pot of heather
10 stems of purple trachelium
trailing and berried ivy
3 small terracotta pots, 5 cm (2 in) high
selection of blackberries, blueberries and horse chestnuts
9 Scotchbell or miniature peppers
florists' scissors

halloween wreath

We often associate autumn with shades of rust, red and terracotta. However, purples and mauves are also predominant at this time of year. Many of the berries and haws are of such a deep purple as to appear almost black. There are also mauve Michaelmas daises, the ornamental cabbage with its fanciful leaves, as pretty as any rose, and of course the glorious purples of heathland heather. Mix this rich autumnal harvest with the vibrant orange of peppers, gourds and Chinese lanterns, and you have a stunning combination for a Halloween wreath.

1 Begin by wiring the peppers and several cabbage leaves. To wire a cabbage leaf, gently break it off at the base of the stem and cut out the core. Pleat the leaf and then, holding the gathered leaf between your finger and thumb, push a stub wire though the central point, so that the pleats are held in place. Bend the wire down and twist the ends together.

2 Soak the wreath base in a bowl of water for a few minutes. Position the peppers equally around the base. Push cabbage leaves into the wreath near the base of the peppers.

3 Add sprigs of heather, berried ivy and trachelium, cut to about 10 cm (4 in) lengths, building up the arrangement around the peppers.

4 Cut the roses 10 cm (4 in) from the head and add in groups of three, fanning away from the peppers. Cut the orchid stems in half and add in the same way.

5 Wire the terracotta pots by pushing a stub wire through the hole in the bottom of the pot and twisting the wire around. Fill with berries and gently push into the wreath.

6 Finish the wreath by adding the wired horse chestnuts, Scotchbell peppers and blackberries.

thanksgiving wreath

MATERIALS

36 cm (14 in) wet foam ring

selection of autumn foliage including blackberries, crab apples, vine leaves, old man's beard, rosehips, cotoneaster

scissors

medium gauge florists' wire

5 bunches small grapes

7 medium shiny red apples

12 *Leonardis* roses

Whether to be used as a tablecentre or a decoration for a font, this large wreath encompasses all the most beautiful aspects of autumn, combining the rich colourful foliage with the fruits and berries available at this celebratory time. The smaller wreath could either be used as a pew end to echo the font or as an individual decoration for each guest's plate which could then be taken home as a thanksgiving present when all the pumpkin pie has been finished!

1 Soak the foam wreath in water for 5 minutes. Cut some sprigs of foliage to 12 cm (4½ in) in length and strip the lower stems of leaves. Starting from the outside, arrange them around the outside edge keeping close to the plastic base and angled slightly down and in a clockwise direction.

2 Using sprigs of foliage 5 cm (2 in) long, arrange them around the inside of the base in an anticlockwise direction.

3 Gradually cover the entire base, adding crab apples, old man's beard, rosehips and blackberries at intervals.

4 Wire the apples and bunches of grapes (see page 113) and push in at equal distances around the wreath. You may find it easier to position these before pushing them into the foam.

5 Finally add the roses, cutting each stem about 12 cm (4½ in) from the head. Arrange them individually or in groups of three around the wreath.

6 If the wreath is to be a table decoration, ensure that some of the roses, apples and grapes are placed around the outside and can be seen by guests once they are seated.

terracotta and dried flower wreath

MATERIALS

6 medium gauge stub wires

old-fashioned terracotta pot

fine gauge stub wires

5 dried mushrooms

5 walnuts

dried rose leaves

16 Chinese lantern heads

12 hazelnuts

5 dried orange slices

5 poppy heads

12 dried chillies

5 achillea heads

florists' wiring tape

glue gun or tube of all-purpose glue

There are so many types of dried flowers around now that if chosen carefully, they can look just as beautiful as fresh flowers, and of course have the advantage of lasting far longer. The inspiration for this garland was taken from the pot it surrounds, echoing the soft hues of the aged terracotta, and highlighting the brighter oranges. With nuts, Chinese lanterns and poppyheads, the overall feel is autumnal. However, the same idea could be worked on any container – a wicker basket, a small tin pail, an unusual shaped cake tin or a tiny Grecian urn, for example.

1 Overlap and twist the medium gauge stub wires together to create a firm circle with the same diameter as the flower pot.

2 Wire each item individually, using fine gauge wire. The achillea should be split into smaller bunches before being wired.

3 Using the florists' tape bind each wired item on to the wire base as you would when making a floral head-dress.

Group the flowers quite tightly together and angle some upwards to cover the wire as you work.

4 When the whole wire circle has been covered, rest it on the rim of the flowerpot and rearrange parts of the garland if necessary to ensure there are no mechanics showing and the garland has an even density all around. Using a glue gun or tube of glue, glue the garland securely to the pot.

bread wreath

MATERIALS

1.5 kg (3 lb/10 cups) strong white flour

20 ml (4 tsp) salt

30 g (1 oz) white vegetable fat

30 g (1 oz) dried yeast

900 ml (1½ pints) tepid water

baking tray

2 beaten eggs

pastry brush

rolling pin

sharp knife

7 cloves

satin varnish and paintbrush (optional)

The bread wreath is a wonderful symbol of continuity, fertility and life. It is strongly associated with harvest time – the reaping of the year's crop and the sowing of the new make a circle of bread a popular offering in many cultures around the world.

1 Combine the flour and salt in a large bowl. Add the fat and rub in well. Stir in the yeast, then add the water and stir to form a soft dough.

2 Turn the dough onto a floured surface and knead for 5 minutes. Return the dough to the bowl, cover with a clean cloth and leave in a warm place to rise for approximately 1 hour.

3 Divide the mixture into three equal portions. Take two portions and cover the third with a damp cloth to prevent it drying out as you work.

4 Roll the two portions together into a sausage approximately 75 cm (30 in) long and 7.5 cm (3 in) wide. Bring the two ends of the sausage round to form a circle. To join them, dab some water on each end and pinch them together.

5 Transfer the wreath to a floured baking tray and reshape if necessary. Brush with beaten egg.

6 Roll out half of the remaining dough to a thickness of 5 mm (¼ in). Keep the dough you are not using covered with a damp cloth. Using a sharp knife, cut out different shaped leaves and stick these to the wreath with beaten egg.

7 Break off small pieces from the last piece of dough and roll out balls roughly 4 cm (1½ in) in diameter to make the apples, and several smaller balls 1 cm (½ in) in diameter to make the bunches of grapes. Arrange these between the leaves, sticking them to the wreath with beaten egg and push in the cloves to represent stems.

8 Place the wreath in a preheated oven at 220°C/425°F/gas 7 and bake for about 30 minutes until well risen and golden brown.

9 When baked, carefully transfer the wreath to a wire rack until completely cool. If you wish to keep this wreath rather than eat it, you can preserve it by painting the whole wreath, front and back, with two coats of varnish. Allow the wreath to dry for at least 24 hours between each coat.

MATERIALS

30 cm (12 in) strips of 5 different types
of checked fabric

heart-shaped card template,
12.5 x 12.5 cm (5 x 5 in)

scissors

pins

needle and thread

wooden buttons, embroidery thread or
ribbon

wadding or cotton wool

pot pourri

household string

2 m (2¼ yards) gingham ribbon

small rag doll

30 cm (12 in) wired wreath base

shaker scented wreath

The Shakers were a religious group that evolved at the beginning of the nineteenth century. Their philosophy was simplicity, purity and unity. This is demonstrated in their furniture and craftsmanship. Today, the Shaker style of furniture, the simple colours and the home-spun feel of their furnishings and bed linen are still very popular. This wreath takes its influence from the Shaker movement, incorporating gingham, appliquéd hearts and natural fabrics. Each little heart and pouch is filled with pot pourri, making this a wonderful wreath to hang in a bedroom or nursery.

1 To make the padded hearts, cut out 18 hearts using the card template. Cut out a further seven slightly smaller hearts in different fabrics.

2 Pin five smaller hearts to five larger hearts and sew around the edge of each. Take two hearts and pin with right sides facing, then sew around the edge. Leave a 5 cm (2 in) gap.

3 Turn right sides out and stuff using a mixture of potpourri and wadding. Ensure the stuffing is pushed right into the corners to give a good shape. Fold in the edges of the fabric and sew up the gap. Each heart can be finished with a wooden button, ribbon or a cross stitch motif if you wish.

4 To make the pouches, cut four strips of fabric, 35 cm (14 in) long and 12.5 cm (5 in) wide. Decorate with hearts, buttons or embroidery. Fold in half, right sides facing, and sew up both sides. Turn inside out and neatly hem the top. Fill the pouches with pot pourri and tie with a piece of ribbon or string.

5 To assemble the wreath, arrange the hearts, pouches and little rag doll around the wreath, alternating the fabrics. Then simply sew these to the wire base.

chilli wreath

MATERIALS

90 cm (36 in) length of plastic-coated
heavy gauge wire

rubber gloves (optional)

40 red chilli peppers

40 fresh bay leaves

pair of strong pliers

several strands of raffia
1.5 m (58 in) long

Inspired by the chilli chains found in the souks around the Middle East, this wreath looks as effective when dried as it does fresh and would make a wonderful present for an enthusiastic cook. The beauty of it is that it is very easy to add more chillies as the wreath becomes depleted.

Chillies are the widest used flavouring in cooking today, being a main ingredient in many Indian, Thai and Mexican dishes. There are over two hundred varieties worldwide – red, green, black, white and orange, skinny, fat, bell-shaped and cherry-like – so the possibilities are endless!

It is advisable to wear rubber gloves when working with chillies (or wash your hands thoroughly afterwards) as their juice can irritate, especially if it gets into your eyes.

1 Bend the wire into a circle. If you are planning to use the chillies for cooking it is advisable to sterilise the wire in boiling water or sterilising liquid before you use it.

2 Wearing rubber gloves, carefully thread alternate chillies and bay leaves onto the wire hoop until you have a complete circle.

3 Using a pair of pliers, bend each end of the wire back to form a small hook.

4 Tie the lengths of raffia into a bow and thread it on to one of the wire hooks. Link the two wire hooks together.

kitchen wreath

With the ever increasing interest in all types of cookery comes an amazing array of unusual kitchen utensils, some very useful, others not so! A selection of the smaller ones, however, makes an amusing display for the kitchen wall. The same principle could be adapted for other themes, such as using tiny books and miniature scrolls to make a library wreath or sample perfume bottles to make a garland for a feminine dressing room.

1 Cover the plastic base of the wreath with masking tape. Make a loop to hang the wreath (see page 115).

2 Position the largest utensils around the base so they are evenly spaced and the colours and textures alternate.

3 Taking each item in turn, attach to the base. With the smaller items use stub wires bent into a hairpin shape, hook them over the item and push into the foam. For the larger items such as the salt and pepper pots, use nylon wire tied around the utensil and then around the wreath base.

4 Cut the tea towels or dish cloths into strips and gently wind them between the kitchen utensils, covering the foam and securing with hairpins of wire as you go.

5 To blow an egg, wash the shell thoroughly and using a darning needle, make a small hole at each end. Push the needle through the egg to break the yolk. Over a bowl, blow through one end until the yolk and the white of the egg have come out. Rinse and dry the egg before using.

6 Finally, add the tea bags, nutmegs and eggs using a glue gun or all-purpose glue.

MATERIALS

4 oranges

5 ping pong balls

5 different types of seeds or pulses

tube of all-purpose glue

sheet of newspaper

strands of raffia

medium gauge stub wires

one box of lichen (available from florists and dried flower suppliers)

30 cm (12 in) floral foam base

reel wire

9 garlic heads

4 bunches of cinnamon sticks

chillies

bay leaves

rosemary

thyme

In many countries a herbal wreath hung in the kitchen or on the door is seen as a sign of welcome and good luck, and always makes a wonderful present, especially for those with culinary interests.

Here I have combined different herbs and spices but you could make a wreath solely of one type of herb. Alternatively, a themed wreath would work well, such as an Indian wreath using different types of dried chillies, saffron, garlic and cardamom pods or an Italian wreath with garlic, sun-dried tomatoes and bunches of dried oregano and thyme.

1 To make the dried oranges, carefully score the skin of the orange through to the flesh and leave overnight in a very low oven or for several days in an airing cupboard until completely dry.

2 To make the spice balls, cover the ping pong balls in glue and then gently roll each of them in a different spice or seeds. Allow to dry thoroughly on a sheet of newspaper before tying with a length of raffia.

3 Using 'U' shaped pins made from medium gauge wire, start by pinning clumps of lichen around the outside of the base, ensuring that you completely cover the plastic base. Continue along the inside and then over the top until the whole wreath is covered.

4 Make a hook at the back of the wreath using a stub wire (see page 115 for method).

5 Wire the garlic heads by pushing two stub wires in a cross at the base of the bulb. Bend the wires back and twist together.

6 Wire up the cinnamon bunches and spice balls (see page 114) and arrange around the top of the wreath. Secure by pushing into the foam base.

7 Wire the chillies and bay leaves and add to the wreath. Finally, position sprigs of rosemary and thyme between the larger items and around the edge.

winter

The stark juxtapositions of winter, from the warmth of log fires to the frost-covered silhouettes of branches on an icy morning, make it a season of many contrasts. Christmas brings a feeling of revelry and celebration, with presents piled under the tree, candles glowing among rosy red apples, spikes of holly and boughs of mistletoe.

MATERIALS

4 church candles

stub wires

oasis tape

5 shiny red apples

5 pine cones

12 walnuts

bunches of cotoneaster berries

30 cm (12 in) foam base

selection of Christmas foliage, such as conifer, blue spruce, rosemary, holly, larch and ivy

secateurs

9 red roses, such as *Grand Prix*

cinnamon sticks

This is a traditional Christmas wreath, encompassing all the fruits, nuts and berries of Christmas with beautiful deep red roses, surrounding four thick cream church candles, one to be lit each week as Christmas draws nearer.

With this wreath, as with a lot of Christmas arrangements, the interest comes from the variety of foliage used, so it is a good idea to take a brisk walk with a pair of secateurs before you start and see if you can collect a wide selection of different types of berries, firs and hollies. You only need a little of each one to provide a wonderfully rich background for the roses.

1 Start by wiring the candles. For each candle, take four stub wires and bend each to form a hairpin. Position these equally around the candle base with the open end of the pin facing down, extending 5 cm (2 in) below the base of the candle. Secure with oasis tape.

2 Next, wire the apples, pine cones and walnuts (see pages 113-114). Wire the cotoneaster berries into small clusters.

3 Soak the wreath base in a bowl of water for a few minutes. Taking different types of foliage, cut into 12.5 cm (5 in) pieces, strip the lower stem clean of leaves, and push them into the outside of the wet foam wreath just above the plastic rim, angled in a clockwise direction all the way round. Do the

same on the inside of the wreath with 5 cm (2 in) lengths of foliage, placing them in an anticlockwise direction.

4 Position the candles equally around the wreath, then add the wired apples and pine cones. Continue to build up the foliage around the candles, apples and pine cones while leaving space for the roses.

5 Cut the rose stems to 10 cm (4 in) and add to the wreath in clusters of three, pushing them into the base. Add cinnamon, cotoneaster berries and walnuts around the candle.

6 If you wish to display the wreath on a surface that could be damaged by water, place it on a tray. With careful watering it should last the whole advent month, with the exception of the roses which should be replaced each week.

gold wreath

From the very first Christmas, when the three kings bought gifts for the new-born Jesus, gold has been associated with celebrations and festivities. This rich, lush wreath would make a wonderful focal point for any Christmas decorations, whether hung on the front door, a wall or used around the base of a candelabra. With its gilded apples, twists of organza and golden cherubs, it makes a truly memorable centrepiece.

MATERIALS

3 large apples, such as Gala apples
cream emulsion paint
paint brush
box, berried ivy and trailing ivy
sharp florists' scissors
30 cm (12 in) wet foam base
50 cm (20 in) gold net
scissors
2 m (2¼ yards) gold ribbon
medium gauge stub wires
2 m (2¼ yards) white organza ribbon
1 m (1 yard) gold organza, cut into three strips
a selection of gold baubles in different sizes
3 gold cherubs
16 small gold candles
3 wooden apples

1 Paint the real apples with cream emulsion and allow to dry.

2 Cut sprigs of box and berried ivy 15 cm (6 in) long. Remove the lower foliage and push the sprigs in all around the outside rim of the wreath.

3 Cut three 36 cm (14 in) squares of net. Wrap each painted apple in net and tie with gold ribbon. Wire each apple. Push the apples into the floral foam, equally spaced around the base.

4 Using hairpins of stub wire to secure them, twist the strips of organza around the wreath.

5 Wire the remaining decorations and arrange around the wreath. Finish by adding a few sprigs of trailing ivy, and a little extra foliage to cover any gaps, particularly on the inside rim.

winter white wreath

After the richness and opulence of Christmas decorations, the cool, pale creams and whites of this wreath make a refreshing antidote. It reflects the clear, frosty winter mornings, the snowy banks and hedgerows covered with puffs of old man's beard. Incorporating the blues and greys so often found in winter foliage, such as the metallic blue of the laurustinus berries, the dusty spheres of the eucalyptus and the charcoal hues of fallen beech leaves, this wreath would make a wonderful centrepiece for a New Year dinner or a winter wedding arrangement.

MATERIALS
8 *Bianca* white roses
5 stems of *Princess* spray rose
5 stems of cream lisianthus
1 bunch of white ranunculus
10 stems of *laurustinus vibernum*
10 stems of eucalyptus
1 bunch of rosemary
5 stems of old man's beard
variegated trailing ivy
35 cm (14 in) wet foam base
15 seed pods
medium gauge stub wires

1 Condition the flowers and foliage as described on pages 110-111. Leave to stand in a cool place for at least 12 hours after cutting. Soak the foam base in water for about 5 minutes. While this is soaking, wire the seed pods.

2 Cut a variety of foliage cut to approximately 15 cm (6 in) in length and start by building up a background of foliage around the outside of the wreath. Do the same around the inside rim using slightly shorter pieces of foliage until the whole base is covered.

3 Begin to add the flowers. Start with the largest, in this case the *Bianca* roses, by arranging them in groups of three. Add the spray roses, ranunculus, seed pods and lisianthus, angling them slightly so they can be seen from every angle.

4 Give the whole wreath a good spray with water and keep in a cool place until it is needed.

leafy wreaths

These wreaths are the perfect antidote to some of the more gaudy decorations you find in the shops at Christmas time. Using solely one type of foliage, each wreath is simple in itself, but when massed together they can look stunning.

Here I have made holly, ivy and laurustinus wreaths, but mistletoe, blue spruce, nuts, pine cones or apple slices would look equally good. The beauty of these wreaths comes from their simplicity.

MATERIALS
20 cm (8 in) wire wreath frame
sphagnum moss
reel wire
holly (ideally with berries), cut to 10 cm (4 in) lengths
sharp florists' scissors
gardening gloves (optional)

holly wreath

1 Soak the sphagnum moss in water for 5 minutes. Gently squeeze the moss to remove some of the excess water. Fill the frame with soaked sphagnum moss and bind it tightly with reel wire to create a solid shape on which to work.

2 Using a double leg mount (see page 112), wire together three or four sprigs of holly at a time.

3 Push each bunch of holly through the moss and out the other side. Bend the wires back on themselves to secure the bunch.

4 Continue adding bunches of holly until the whole wreath is covered. This method could also be used for blue spruce, fir or rosemary.

laurustinus wreath

MATERIALS
20 cm (8 in) foam wreath base
2 stub wires
sprigs of laurustinus, cut to 7.5 cm (3 in)
in length

1 Soak the wreath in a sink of water for approximately 5 minutes.

2 Twist the stub wires together, then twist around the wreath base and form a loop at the top of the base (see page 115). This will make a hook from which to hang the wreath.

3 Take sprigs of laurustinus and strip each of its bottom leaves, then push them into the foam base around the outer edge. Position each one slightly down and at a 45 degree angle away from the wreath in a clockwise direction, taking care to cover the plastic base.

4 Repeat this on the inside of the wreath using slightly shorter pieces of foliage. Angle these laurustinus sprigs in an anticlockwise direction.

5 Finally, build up the foliage in the centre of the wreath, ensuring it is quite densely packed to create impact, and to guarantee none of the florists' foam shows. You could also use this method for berried ivy, mistletoe and more delicate foliage that needs a good supply of water.

ivy leaf wreath

MATERIALS
15 cm (6 in) dry foam wreath
ivy leaves
packet of steel dressmakers' pins
pair of florists' scissors

1 Select different sized ivy leaves and cut each one off at the stem right at the base of the leaf.

2 Start by pinning one ivy leaf on the top of the base, then add an ivy leaf either side, pinning the leaf to the base using two pins per leaf. Continue until the width of the wreath is covered.

3 Any leaves that overlap the edge should be tucked under and pinned on the back to create a neat edge.

4 Keep working in small sections around the wreath, overlapping each leaf over the last and taking care to cover the pins as you work.

5 Continue until the entire wreath is covered. When you come full circle, lift the tips of the first leaves and tuck the bottoms of the last leaves under before pinning. This ensures a neat, continuous circle of leaves. You could use this method for laurel leaves, or spray ivy leaves gold and add a wired gold ribbon bow for a more festive wreath.

mulled wine wreath

MATERIALS

6 large oranges

sharp knife

greaseproof paper

baking tray

medium gauge stub wires

5 kumquats

packet of cloves

few strands of raffia

50 cm (20 in) strip of muslin

1 small packet cotton wool

1 m (1 yard) household string

4 squares of silk 25 x 10 cm (10 x 4 in)

needle and matching thread

2 m (2¼ yards) satin ribbon

12 cinnamon sticks

42 cm (17 in) vine base

5 spice balls (see Dried Herb wreath on page 79)

9 whole nutmegs

glue gun or tube of all-purpose glue

'Sugar and spice and all things nice.' There is something about the smell of mulled wine that immediately conjures up thoughts of Christmas, of mince pies, open fires and carols. This wreath takes all the elements of a traditional mulled wine and combines them to make a Christmas wreath that is a little different. It would be wonderful hung in the kitchen to capture the aromatic scents throughout the festive season.

1 Cut two oranges in half and gently remove all the flesh and pith, leaving just the peel intact. Slice a third orange and arrange the slices and orange shells on a baking tray covered with greaseproof paper. Leave overnight in a very low oven or for several days in an airing cupboard to dry out thoroughly. When dry, wire the orange slices together in groups of three.

2 Stud the remaining oranges and a few kumquats with cloves. Tie the remaining kumquats with raffia. Wire the oranges and kumquats (see page 113).

3 For the bouquet garni, cut out 10 circles of muslin, approximately 15 cm (6 in) in diameter. Take two circles of muslin and fill with cottonwool, then tie with a piece of string. Continue until all five bouquets garnis are made.

4 To make the silk pouches, fold the fabric in half, right sides facing, and sew up each side. Turn inside out and stuff with cottonwool. Gather the top together and tie with a ribbon bow.

5 Wire cinnamon sticks in groups of four. Conceal the wire with ribbon.

6 Once you have assembled all the 'ingredients', arrange them in groups around the wreath starting with the oranges. Add the cinnamon sticks, kumquats, silk pouches, and orange slices. Attach with stub wires, making sure they are pushed right through the wreath and bent back to secure them.

7 Finally, use a glue gun or all-purpose adhesive to attach the orange peel, bouquet garni and spice balls.

sequin wreath

This wonderful shiny, jewelled wreath is a treasure you would find in an Aladdin's cave. It is so pretty you could hang it on the wall just as it is or frame it against crushed velvet in a deep gilt frame. If you are feeling extravagant you could make several wreaths and hang them with beautiful organza ribbon from the Christmas tree to sparkle and catch the light as they swing from the branches. Beads or buttons would also work equally well.

MATERIALS

15 cm (6 in) dry foam or polystyrene base

50 cm (20 in) organza ribbon (optional)

2 tins of glass or pearl-headed dressmakers' pins

large selection of sequins in different sizes, shapes and colours

1 If you wish to hang this wreath from the tree, loop a piece of organza ribbon around the base and tie in a knot. Pin the knot at the back of the wreath so that it does not show.

2 Working in small sections, select different shaped and coloured sequins and arrange them around the wreath base. Work from the inner and outer sides up to the top of the wreath. Allow some to overlap, and secure each one with a pin as you work.

3 Continue until the whole wreath is covered, making sure the colours and shapes are well spread out.

MATERIALS

2 m (2¼ yards) paper ribbon

30 cm (12 in) foam wreath base

sticky tape

4 pieces of card 7.5 x 7.5 cm (3 x 3 in)

6 sheets of brightly coloured paper

12 empty matchboxes

4 small gift boxes

selection of different coloured ribbons
60 cm (24 in) long in a variety of widths

medium gauge stub wires

6 gift tags

2 ready-made present rosettes

1 m (1 yard) wired ribbon,
7.5 cm (3 in) wide

present wreath

This wreath is a novel alternative to traditional Christmas crackers. It works along the same lines – everyone receives a present, and you could always add a hat and joke too. The wreath could either be hung on your door to greet guests as they arrive or be placed on the table as a centrepiece. The presents could be anything from indoor fireworks, luxurious hand-made chocolates, humorous gifts or something altogether more lavish. Whatever the gift, when presented like this it is bound to be memorable!

1 Unravel the paper ribbon and wrap it around the wreath base, overlapping the edges to ensure the wreath is entirely covered. Secure the ends on the underside of the wreath with sticky tape.

2 Roll each piece of card into a cylinder and secure with sticky tape. Fill the boxes and cardboard tubes with your chosen presents.

3 Neatly wrap each box and tube in the wrapping paper, tying each one with corresponding ribbon.

4 Push a stub wire underneath the back of each present's ribbon, bend the wire in half and twist together to form two prongs. Push these firmly into the wreath base to secure the presents. Add the presents at different angles around the wreath, leaving a space at the bottom for the bow. Take care not to put boxes of the same paper or size too close to each other.

5 Tie on the gift tags, stick on the present rosettes and finish the wreath with a large wired bow.

useful tools

These are the tools that have been used in this book. Many are not essential but simply make life a lot easier! However, a good pair of scissors and stub wires are a must, and a glue gun is also very useful.

DOUBLE-SIDED TAPE OR STICKY PADS: Available from DIY stores or stationers, these are ideal for attaching light objects, particularly when gluing would not be suitable.

FLORISTS' TAPE: The advantage of florists' tape is that it is green and therefore easily camouflaged. It is water-resistant and relatively strong, making it suitable for wiring candles, taping floral foam and covering large wires.

GLOVES: A good pair of gardening gloves is extremely useful when dealing with materials such as holly, brambles or roses, or chillies which can irritate the skin. If you find it difficult to work with such gloves, thin latex ones offer some protection, and are much easier to wear when handling fiddly things.

GLUE GUN: Many wreaths in this book were made using a glue gun -- an electric 'gun' that melts sticks of glue. Although you can use a tube of normal all-purpose adhesive, a glue gun has the advantage of drying, and therefore sticking, instantly. It is capable of sticking almost anything and is well worth investing in if you plan to make many craft items.

MASKING TAPE: This is always useful to have, and you will be amazed how often it comes in handy. In this book I have used it for jobs as diverse as covering the green plastic base of a wreath and securing a dry foam base to its backing.

NYLON WIRE: Available from display shops, this is an invisible wire that is capable of holding fairly heavy weights. In this book I have used it where it is important that wire is not visible and gluing would not be practical, for example on many of the utensils in the kitchen wreath.

PLIERS: Useful for cutting wire, or to bend and shape wire.

RAFFIA: Not only does raffia look wonderful tied around cinnamon sticks or in large bows on a rustic arrangement, it is also very useful for tying smaller objects.

REEL WIRE: Fairly self-explanatory, this is also known as mossing wire and is used to bind moss to wreaths and also for making garlands.

RIBBON: There are so many wonderful types of ribbon available now – wired, paper, silk taffeta, tartan and organza. One length can make all the difference to your wreath. It is worth looking out for some of the more unusual ones.

SCISSORS: A good, sharp pair of scissors are invaluable for any floristry work. Available from flower shops, dried flower and sundry shops or large department stores and garden centres. It is important to keep your scissors sharp and not use them for cutting wire which blunts them very quickly.

SECATEURS: To cut woody stems.

SPRAYER: This is essential if you are working with fresh flowers as they are capable of taking in almost as much water though their petals and leaves as their stems. Frequent spraying will ensure the flowers stay looking fresh for much longer, particularly with wired flowers such as head-dresses where this is the only form of water intake they have. They are cheap to buy from garden centres.

STUB WIRES: Although there are several types of gauged wires, the most commonly used are 20/22/28 and 30. The 20 gauge is useful for wiring heavy flowers such as sunflowers, fruit and nuts. Gauge 22 is what I have referred to as medium gauge wire throughout the book and is most commonly used as it is ideal for wiring roses, bunches of flowers and pine cones. Gauges 28 and 30 are finer gauges and useful for stitching leaves and delicate flowers, such as lily of the valley, bluebells and stephanotis.

WIRING TAPE: This can either be made from thin plastic or paper and comes in green, brown and white. It is used to neaten the stems after a flower, leaf or fruit has been wired, or for taping garland head-dresses and other fine bridal work. For most purposes here the green tape is preferable, though brown is useful for dried flowers.

wreath bases

There are several different types of wreath bases that have been used in this book. Many can be bought from dried flower and florists' supply shops, or if you have a good relationship with your local flower shop they may be able to supply you with some of the more unusual materials.

However, even though the ready-made bases do save time, there is nothing to stop you making your own. Here is an outline of the bases used in this book, plus instructions for making the most commonly used ones.

wet foam base

Wet foam bases are invaluable when arranging fresh flowers and foliage. Consisting of a circular plastic tray filled with florists' foam, they are available in various diameters ranging from 20 cm (8 in) up to 46 cm (18 in). They are also available in diamond and heart shapes, as used in the Valentine's day wreath.

Although they are not very successful when reused as a fresh base, they can be dried out and covered to be used as a base for wreaths such as the summer berry wreath or the sweet wreath.

chicken wire and floral foam base

This serves the same use as manufactured wet foam bases. Chicken wire is available from DIY stores, garden centres and builders' merchants. You will need the small 2.5 cm (1 in) holed wire if you can get it.

1 To make a 30 cm (12 in) wreath, soak a block of florists' foam in water for about 3 minutes and then cut it into several rectangular cubes 5 cm (2 in) square and 7.5 cm (3 in) long.

2 Cut a length of chicken wire 1 m (1 yard) long and 15 cm (6 in) wide. Lay the blocks of floral foam along the chicken wire, leaving a small gap between each one to enable you to bend the wreath into a circle.

3 Take a strip of black plastic bin liner 5 cm (2 in) wide and 1 m (1 yard) long and lay it on top of the floral foam.

4 Bringing the two sides up, 'sew' together the chicken wire using a length of reel wire.

5 Bend the sausage round to form a circle and join the ends together with reel wire.

6 If you wish to make a firmer base, back the wreath as described on page 110. However, instead of using all-purpose glue, bind the wreath to the base with reel wire.

dry foam bases

Made from a stiff brown foam, these bases are ideal for any dried wreath, whether it be dried flowers or sequins. They are available in various diameters from 15 cm (6 in) to 30 cm (12 in). These bases are fairly fragile and are best backed if you are planning to use heavy materials.

wire frame

Useful for many types of wreath, this versatile frame is particularly handy when you simply need a circular base. Both the Shaker and lavender wreaths in this book were made using one of these. They are available in several sizes and are inexpensive to buy.

moss base

This is a wire frame filled with sphagnum moss and useful for fresh wreaths as an alternative to the wet foam base. It has the advantage of being lighter and is therefore easy to hang from a nail or door knob.

1 To make a moss base, soak 5 large handfuls of sphagnum moss in a bucket of water for about 5 minutes.
2 Squeeze the moss to remove any excess water and pack the moss fairly tightly into the wire frame.
3 Bind the moss to the wreath using reel wire.
4 Trim off any loose strands of moss to give a solid base on which to work.

plaster base

This creates a firm base for heavy materials, such as the mosaic wreath.

1 To make a plaster base, pack a wire frame tightly with crumpled newspaper and tape it in place with masking tape.

2 Dip strips of calico 5 cm (2 in) wide and approximately 30 cm (12 in) long in a runny solution of plaster of Paris.

3 Wind the strips around the base until all the newspaper is covered.

4 Allow to dry before repeating with two further layers of calico dipped in plaster, again leaving the plaster to dry between each layer.

straw base

This is a good, cheap alternative to a dry foam base or a moss and wire base. It is made using the same method as the twig base by bunching handfuls of straw or hay together and binding with reel wire to make a 'snake' of straw. Trim any excess loose strands. Finally, mould the base into a circular shape, then join the ends together with reel wire.

plastic and plastic-covered hoops

These are available from florists' supply shops or, for the larger hoops, you could use a child's plastic hula hoop. These are designed for a base for bridesmaid's hoop, although they can be used for any wreath that requires a light, two-dimensional base. The smaller bases can easily be made with heavy gauge galvanised wire covered in florists' tape. These bases are used for the chilli wreath and the sunflower wreath.

twig base

This base is easy to make and suitable for wreaths where the materials do not require water, such as the feather or mulled wine wreaths. These twig wreaths also look very attractive on their own when made from unusual materials such as twisted willow, vines, rope or even barbed wire. If you find it difficult to bend the twigs, most will become more pliable if soaked in water.

1 To make a twig base, gather together a handful of twigs of roughly the same length.

2 Taking another bundle of similar thickness, position it approximately halfway along the first length of twigs. Bind the two together with reel wire.

3 Gently bend the twigs into a circular shape and continue adding new bundles at similar intervals, and binding them with the wire as you go, until you have the required size wreath.

4 Join the two ends together and bind with reel wire.

conditioning fresh materials

It is important when arranging any flowers or foliage to condition them before you use them as this greatly enhances their lifespan. It also firms up their stems which is particularly important if they are to be arranged in florists' foam where they cannot drink freely. In addition, it prevents flowers wilting prematurely. To ensure longevity of flowers once they have been conditioned, spray with a fine mist of water and keep in a cool, draught-free environment. Top up arrangements regularly.

Flowers: Most flowers simply need to have their stems cut at a 45 degree angle and any foliage around the bottom of the stems removed. Then place in deep water, approximately 10 cm (4 in) from their heads for at least 12 hours. It is a good idea to add a commercial flower food or a combination of 1 capful of household bleach and 15 ml (1 tablespoon) of sugar to each bucket.

Roses: Some flowers, such as roses, can develop air locks in their stems which prevent them from taking up water and therefore cause the heads to droop. To remedy this, place the cut stems in boiling water for up to 2 minutes, holding the heads away from the steam. Wrap the heads firmly in damp newspaper before placing in deep water, again for at least 12 hours.

Tulips: Tulips often bend and flop if not given support while being conditioned, so wrap the stems and heads in newspaper before conditioning them. Remember that tulips continue to grow after being cut, so if you are using them in an arrangement with other flowers, cut the tulips a little shorter than necessary.

Daffodils: Some flowers such as daffodils and euphorbias produce a sticky substance from their stems when cut, so it is better to condition these separately.

Foliage: Most foliage can be conditioned in a similar way to flowers, although woody stems need to be flattened with a hammer before immersing in water.

wiring

For many of the wreaths featured in this book it is necessary to wire the materials before you use them. By wiring a item you give it a firm stem, i.e. a wire with which to attach it to the wreath, whether you are taping it as in the garland method or sticking it into a floral foam base.

Many different types of materials can be wired successfully. Here are examples of the items used in this book. However by using these techniques you could wire up most natural materials. When wiring most flowers it is easiest if you cut the stems about 2.5 cm (1 in) from the flower head.

Double leg mount: The most commonly used wiring technique is the double leg mount which serves to strengthen floral stems, wire heavy-headed flowers and is also useful for bunching together mixed flowers and foliage, as in the sunflower wreath for example.

Place a medium gauge wire along the stem of the flower so that approximately two-thirds of the wire is above the base of the stem and a third is below it. Bend the longer end of the wire down to form a hairpin. Now twist the longer end around the stem and the shorter piece of wire, leaving two wires of equal length.

Single leg mount: Useful for more delicate flowers or when making head-dresses and garlands, where each single flower needs to be wired up.

Bend a piece of medium gauge wire approximately one third of the way along the wire to form a 'U' shape. Line the cut stem up with the shorter wire

and twist the long wire around both the stem and the shorter wire to leave one long 'leg'.

Stitching a leaf: Taking a fine gauge wire, thread it through the main vein of the leaf about halfway up so that the wire is almost invisible from the front, bend the wires down and twist around the stem. If you want a particularly firm stem, add half a medium gauge wire at the base of the leaf, and twist the fine gauge wires around this too.

Push a medium gauge stub wire though the base of the fruit. Then push another wire though the base to form a cross. Bend the wires down and twist all four together. With some more delicate fruit and vegetables, such as Brussels sprouts or chillies, it is possible to use just one wire, bending it down and twisting the two prongs together.

Wiring a rose: This method can also be used for gerbera, scabious, tulips and most other single-headed flowers. I find this technique also works well for strawberries and cape gooseberries.

Cut the stem about 2.5 cm (1 in) from the head. Cut a medium gauge stub wire in half and gently push one end up through the stem into the head, being careful not to break the flower. Push a fine gauge wire through the rose head at the base of the flower. Twist the fine wires down and around the medium gauge wire and cover with tape.

Hollow stems: Some stems, such as daffodils, delphiniums and amaryllis, benefit from having their stems strengthened by pushing a stub wire up through the centre of the stem.

Fruit and Vegetables: This method serves most types of vegetables and fruit, in particular apples, oranges, lemons, turnips, pineapples or any fairly solid fruit or vegetable that has a round base.

Berries: To wire individual berries, use a toothpick or half a cocktail stick or a piece of medium gauge stub wire and push the broken end gently into the berry. Fruit which has been wired in this way should not be eaten.

Moss: All moss can be very easily attached to florists' foam by using hairpins of medium gauge wire.

Candles: Take two medium gauge stub wires and cut each in half. Bend these to form four hairpins. Place these around the base of the candle with the open end down. Half the pin should be below the base of the candle. Secure the wires with florists' tape.

Nuts: Drill a small hole at the base of the nut. (With walnuts this is not necessary as they have a soft point at the base.) Gently push in half a medium gauge stub wire as far as it will go and secure it by adding a little glue around the hole.

Eggs: Blown eggs (see page 33) can be wired in a similar way to nuts.

Pine cones: Using a medium gauge stub wire, twist it tightly around the base of the pine cone and then twist the two ends together.

Sweets: Cut a stub wire in half and twist each wire around the twisted part of the sweet wrapper.

Presents: To wire the presents, lay a stub wire along the back of the present and tape it with sticky tape before bending back the ends to make two prongs suitable for pushing into florists' foam.

backing a dried wreath

If you are using heavy materials on your wreath, such as shells or sweets, it will be necessary to back your wreath if you wish to hang it on the wall, not only to provide a base for the hook but also to strengthen the whole structure.

1 Take the wreath base and using this as your template, draw around it onto a piece of hardboard or thick card.

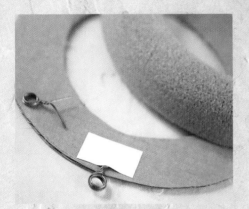

2 Cut out the board using a hacksaw or scissors if using card. Bend two pieces of medium gauge wire around a pen to form a hoop and using strong all-purpose glue or tape, stick this to the hardboard. Allow to dry completely.

3 When dry, stick the board to the dry foam base using all-purpose glue and reinforce by binding the base and board together with masking tape.

making a hook for a wet foam wreath

Though invaluable for arranging fresh flowers and foliage into a wreath, these bases do not have any form of hook should you wish to hang your wreath from the wall or door. However, making one is very simple. These wreath bases hold a lot of water when first soaked so it is advisable to protect your wall or door with a piece of plastic or bin liner placed behind the wreath, at least initially.

1 Take two medium gauge wires. Bend them twice around a pen to form a loop.

2 Wind the two ends firmly around the base and twist together. Trim the wires close to the wreath base.

3 Cover the loop with florists' tape to neaten and protect the wire from rusting and to cover any sharp, protruding ends.

bows

There are two basic type of bow, one is a simple bow, the other a 'looped' bow. Bows can be made from a wide range of materials -- ribbons, raffia, paper, fabric, trailing ivy or vines are just a few suggestions. Whatever you use, they can be used to stunning effect on wreaths of all types.

Simple bow: For wreaths of the size in this book, 1.5 m (5 feet) is normally a suitable length to use to make a 20 cm (8 in) bow However, it is better to allow a slightly longer piece, rather than end up with a ribbon that is too short and therefore wasted.

1 Take a piece of the ribbon approximately one third of the way along and fold it to form a loop,

2 Twist the ribbon around the base of the loop and tuck it through to form another loop, as if for a normal bow, such as when tying a shoe lace.

3 Neaten the ends by cutting the ribbon at an angle, or 'fishtailing' the ends. To do this, fold the ribbon in half widthways before cutting it at an angle. When you open out the ribbon you will have a 'V' shaped end.

Looped bow: For this type of bow you will need a longer piece of ribbon, approximately 3 m (3½ yards) for a similar sized bow.

1 Begin in the same way by making a loop in the ribbon approximately 30 cm (12 in) from one end. Now bend the ribbon around to make a figure of eight.

2 Continue until you have three or four loops on each side, holding the ribbon in a 'pinch point' between your forefinger and thumb in the centre. You should have a 'tail' roughly 30 cm (12 in) long.

3 Taking a shorter piece of the same ribbon, approximately 20 cm (8 in) in length, tie this around the centre of your figure of eight. Neaten the ends by cutting at an angle or 'fishtail'.

4 To wire both ribbons, simply push a piece of medium gauge stub wire though the back of the bow and twist the ends together.

presenting wreaths

Any of the wreaths in this book would make a wonderful present. There is something particularly nice about receiving a gift that has been designed with the recipient in mind. The dried herb or chilli wreath would make a popular present for a keen cook, or a wreath made from miniature books, bookmarks and pens for an author, sewing items for a tailor – the possibilities are only as limited as the imagination!

Which ever wreath you decide to make, the way in which you present it can make all the difference. Many of the wreaths in this book are quite fragile, so it is important that they are boxed properly. A low square or rectangular box is ideal. Flatish boxes used for packing fruit and vegetables are often available at supermarkets, or the lids of boxes used for transporting commercially grown flowers also work well. Often thrown out by flower shops, it is worth asking if they could save a couple for you.

1 Once you have found a lid the right size to hold your wreath, cover it in a plain or printed paper. If you find a paper that complements the colours or theme of the wreath, even better.

2 Line the lid with loosely crumpled tissue paper. Gently lay the wreath in the centre. Cover the top with clear cellophane, taping the edges down with sticky tape.

3 Tie a ribbon round the box and a gift tag that matches the wreath, for example tuck a feather into the bow of the feather wreath or a gold-sprayed leaf on white card for the gold wreath.

Suppliers

Fred Aldous
P O Box 135
37 Lever Street
Manchester 1
M60 1UX
Tel: 0161 236 2477
Fax: 0161 236 6075
Craft materials by mail order.

D.Z.D.
145 Tottenham Court Road
London W1
Tel: 0171 388 7488
For nylon wire, Christmas decorations, staple guns and props. Mail order service available.

Homebase stores
Head Office: Ropley Way
The Hyde
London NW4 6SS
Tel: 0181 200 7500
For chicken wire, glue guns, secateurs, plants and wire.

John Lewis stores
Head Office: 171 Victoria Street
London SW1E 5NN
Tel: 0171 828 1000
For all haberdashery, kitchen equipment and fabrics.

Partridges
132-134 Sloane Street
London SW1
Tel: 0171 730 0651
For quail and duck eggs, unusual spices and vegetables.

Something Special
263-265 London Road
Mitcham
Surrey
Tel: 0181 687 0128
For wet and dry wreath bases, florists' tape, stub wires and all florists' sundries.

Specialist Crafts Ltd
P O Box 247
Leicester LE1 9QS
Tel: 0116 251 0405
Fax: 0116 251 5015
Craft materials by mail order.

Acknowledgements

With thanks to Ron, whose fabulous cakes make it worth getting up so early on Monday mornings! And to everybody at John Austin and Company Ltd.

Thank you to Dave, David and Graham at A & F Bacons.

Thank you to Sandra Lane, for her wonderful interpretation of the wreaths in this book, for being so brilliant to work with and whose ability to make even the most basic step-by-step pictures look interesting never ceased to amaze me!

To Ros Jones, Kate Rowland, Jo and Risto Gronmark, Edward Butler, Clare Baker, John Charlton and Fiona and Christopher Morrison for all their help and encouragement.

Also to my parents who have supported me so enthusiastically from the very beginning of Tiger Rose.

And to Philip, without whom I would never have started Tiger Rose and who has been there constantly, through the highs and lows and never doubted me. Thank you .

Index